# ALIGHT IN THE LAMENT

# ALIGHT IN THE LAMENT

STEVE BROPHY

*Leslie Lau, Benny Wallington*

Signature Sound

# Contents

## 1
## NIGREDO: THE BLACKENING

1. Lost — 2
2. The Underworld — 6
3. The Descent — 13
4. Dark Dawns — 27
5. Perturbation — 36

## 2
## ALBEDO - THE WHITENING

6. The Ascent — 42
7. Relatedness — 49
8. Union — 58

## 3
## RUBEDO - THE REDDENING

| 9 | Love's Fire | 66 |
| 10 | Bibliography | 69 |
| 11 | Acknowledgments | 71 |

# I

# Nigredo: The Blackening

*"When we truly open our hearts to each other, there is no burden too heavy for us to carry together, there is no pain too deep for us to hold in each other's arms. And it's in that place—of feeling the Earth's injuries, and feeling it with each other—that the alchemy emerges. It's in the cauldron of sharing our grief with our community, of gazing at it together and not looking away, that the heartbreak turns to hope."*

*JEREMY LENT*

# I

# Lost

The story is uniquely mine. Yet, like all stories, you will situate yourself within. For there are synergies between my journey and yours. Peaks, Troughs. Blue skies, Storms. Patterns with textures that feel familiar. Smooth in parts, jagged in others.

An unfurling work in progress.
We are perpetual works in progress, fumbling along the path, clambering for meaning. The pages here are devoid of answers. Just acknowledgment.
And by acknowledgment, I mean the original meaning, 'to confess'.

\* \* \*

**A confession.**

The words that adorn these pages are moments in time. They are belay points. Moments that mattered. Poetic transmissions entwined in the unfurling of growth, death, and rebirth.

At times, a story. At times, a poem. An honest confession of language. A symbiosis of prose and verse to honour transmission.

Poetry is a language vessel. Words flow freely in moments of deep stillness. The sound among the stillness allows a fragile unearthing. Exposing deep wells of emotion and experience that lie dormant within. Like a pause between breaths, the tranquil stillness heeds a call to commune. A call to *"commune union"*. Where poetry's role is to language the felt sense. My role is to hold still long enough to provide genesis for the reverence of exiled moments. To pay tribute to moments via the song of language.

A hero of mine, Dr. Martin Shaw, calls poetry *"the language of the exiled."* A language I have only recently come to know...

Recently exiled. It was a call that began the exile. A call that exiled me from an existential sleepwalk that was my life.

Without recognition, many moments in our lives slip by. Lost in the annals of time due to distraction or categorised insignificance. But there are those moments; visceral time travel moments, available to us in half the blink of an eye. The moments that shift the trajectory of our path. Etched deeply in our psyche, where time slows to a crawl, where the silence births salience. Moments we re-memory, over and over and over and over again.

Mine was a Friday afternoon.

My beige hangover nursed by a belly full of chicken nuggets. The quintessential PE teacher's lunch as fuel, I was setting up the softball diamond for Inter-school sport. As the thud of the third base hit the ground, I felt the haptic buzz on my thigh. Distracted by the arrival of the opposing school's bus, I let it go. Swallowing a gulp of fresh air to help the seediness subside, honouring it with a nuggety belch, I pressed on with my duties.

Again, the incessant buzz...
Reaching into my pocket I noticed a slew of missed calls. The new Samsung phone, so confusing. Oh, how I yearned for my trusty Nokia 3310. Looking at the screen, I saw four missed calls in close proximity from Dad.
It rang again...
This time, Aidan flashed up - my younger brother. As I answered, the sun hit me with all its glory. I closed my eyes to be swept up by the magical July day.

***"Hey mate, what's up?"***

## *Mourning strangle*

*Haptic doorways
lead to forever moments
of cataclysmic impact.
Where scorched lines in grass
mask underworld abductions.
The reign of blood-soaked tears,
time travel anchor points
available in an eye blink,
lead to the mourning strangle
we hope morning will forget,
but know gasping grasps
cannot escape
the stark of this dark.
If I don't answer,
does it change his/story?*

# 2

# The Underworld

*"In Western cultures, we rarely enter the underworld except when abducted, by a great loss or depression."*

**BILL PLOTKIN - SOULCRAFT**

Death abducts us into the underworld. Violent theft into a world of darkness, gasping for air, throbbing in trauma as deep physical sobs lash our bones with hurt.

That moment is etched deeply into this heart of mine. Written with a stab of language and a primal scream. But the pain was not yet done with me. It's only now as a father of two, that I know a parent's love. The tsunami of unconditional love that threatens to tear you apart with reverence, fear, and hope. A love you'd give your life for. A life you'd exhale your last breath to protect.

The broken cries of my father still wells me with tears, the ripple of a breaking heart, felt in the deep sobs only grief can surface. The strongest man in my world brought to his knees with the heaviest of words.

**"*Kev's dead.*"**

I still flinch when writing these two words. Their vibration still visceral when they leave my mouth. Hearing them is one thing. Carrying the knife of these words to my mother's ear was another. I must confess. I can never forgive my brother for that. I know he'd understand.

The womb that brought us both to life, died in my arms as the news met her ears.

\* \* \*

## *Womb tears*

*Womb tears give you life,*
*crying as you departed for the first time*
*Desperately hoping for your first tears*

*to gasp you alive*
*But now my womb weeps*
*With the news of your second departure*
*The life I breathed into you*
*blown out with your last breath*
*I die with these words in my heart*


Death is one of life's non-negotiables.

While we may cover our ears when the topic of our own death arises we know the inevitable lurks in our shadows. We can accept that one day we must turn and face the threshold of no return. But seeing a 21-year-old in the prime of his life lying lifeless in a morgue is just something I still find hard to come to terms with.

There he lay in his best suit, his body rigid and wounded. His hair, once a vanity measure of pride, was not the same. It didn't feel the same as I ran my fingers through it. He didn't look the same. Staring back at me was a lifeless vessel. A lifeless vessel that once contained so much spirit.

My heart broke again that day.

As the eldest of four, Kev was our baby brother. There were seven years between us so I had a front-row seat to his entry, all his big moments, and now his exit from this life. I don't really remember crying much before he died. But I could not restrain the violent sobs of my broken heart. I could not restrain the tears of anguish. I cried for the fear he must have felt in his last moments. Scared cries I would hear in my nightmares. I cried as only an older sibling can for being unable to protect him in his time of need. I cried because I would never hear that laugh again. A laugh that escaped through a crooked smile and lit up the world. A crooked smile I would never have the joy of witnessing again.

Grief took the rug out from under my feet, revealing with a harsh permanence the temperance and fragility of the breath we take for granted. I was lost. The gift of the humble breath, a timeless currency we often spend with frivolity, was snuffed out in one fell swoop. A fate we will all face. The gift will run its course. But for some, it's earlier than expected. For some, deeply unexpected.

* * *

### The First Death

*The first death*
*unveils the weakness,*
*the immortal cracks.*
*Spiralling in anxiety,*

*the inevitability
swallows every breath.
The long shadow left,
brings the highest
magnitude of fear.*

*The show will end.
The show will end.*

*In desperation,
we mask;
accolades,
vices,
denial.
Grand plans and elixirs
sought to keep the house of cards
from the Gods.*

*But we get to die;
we get to die
imprinted on the souls
of others;
formless,
eternal.
Life in fear
is death in life.
Fear not,
the dying will come.*

Looking back I find it hard to capture the experience in words. To language the hurt. The dust from the impact blackened the landscape of my life, blinding me. I lost all sense. Everything destabilised. I didn't know how to be in life without him. I didn't know how to act in life without him. Desperate and destructive, I tore at the fabric of everything I once held dear. Life revealed its hand as a house of constructed cards laid at my feet. The valuables, the once revered, revealed their true nature. The veil of who I believed myself to be was nothing but a fable of deceit.

Everything felt false.

A falseness only heartbreak reveals. In the stories I told myself about the world I saw only the hollow. A slew of ill-fitting suits. The false pretences that I previously held with such regard were exposed for their insignificance.

\* \* \*

## *Suits*

*Grabbing at the collar*
*of this ill-fitting suit.*
*Agitation gnawing*

*with narratives of old.*
*Is it too small?*
*Too big?*
*My skin flares,*
*a rebellious cry for help,*
*for reprieve from the artificial*
*essence of a life in disregard.*
*Vices prop this fracturing soul*
*but they can't hide the splinters*
*of against the grain.*
*The existential sinkhole beckons.*
*At the edge of the vortex,*
*light leaks in through cracks,*
*providing a glimmer of hope.*
*The suit,*
*one of many in the closet of supposed success*
*digs in*
*as the wrestle begins.*

# 3

# The Descent

Every morning, I woke with hope in my heart. Could it all have been a dream? Maybe the morning would vanquish the mourning. But every day I died to the reality of life without him. My daily death journey. A descent into darkness that threatened to swallow me whole. I'm not proud of this period. I tried everything to douse the pain. But it only fuelled the torment. I wanted to set myself alight. Drowning in the hurt, I could only gasp for fleeting moments of escape. Moments of inebriation provided a slither of reprieve but in the end, made it all worse. I couldn't drink away the pain or escape the hurt with highs. The pain was waiting for me with fervour on the other side of momentary reprieves.

I was
*alight with lament.*

Six months after Kev's death, my wife (then fiancé) and I moved to Brazil to live. An adventure of a lifetime already in motion before that day, it was a move shadowed by grief. More time to sit, to wallow, just added to the agony spiral. The darkness followed me across the seas. There was no escaping this shadow.

To my darling wife, I thank you from the bottom of my heart for gripping with all of your ferocity the threads of fabric that were us. You saved my life with a love that counteracted the pain.

Tears wrote these words.

\* \* \*

## *Weathered*

*To run or mask the hurt?*
*Nothing works.*
*It just becomes a tighter noose.*
*A heavier weight.*
*Only when we stand*
*in the quagmire of hurt*

*and fully digest our grief*
*will the quicksand let you go.*
*Boy, will you have the scars to show for it!*
*Weathered wisdom*
*gained only in the stark cold of a winter frost,*
*deep in the belly of the beast.*
*The only way out*
*is to weather the storm*
*My storm*
*My story*
*I'm sorry*

Grief had me in the crucible. The love I had for my brother was having its way with me. As I knew it, the alchemical lead of life was dissolving and I was dying with it.

Dying to the old.

Little did I know, amongst death and decay, a magical rebirth, was now underway.

A journey as old as time was unraveling.

And such journeys speak in symbols.

Symbolically this journey is represented in myth and story by the butterfly, a symbol I hold in deep reverence. We mourned for Kev through the brisk air of a biting 2006

Australian winter. His blood spilled on Highway 15, Greensboro, Georgia. The result of a head-on crash during a freak summertime storm in the United States.

He died with light on his face while we held winter in our hearts.

Wintertime in the life cycle of the butterfly is chrysalis time. Unaware of the journey ahead, the caterpillar is dying to the old by digesting itself within the cocoon. The cold winter is time for hiding away for deep inner work. Surprisingly during this cold Winter period, we were inundated with butterflies. The symbol of transformation was everywhere. While such synchronicity could be interpreted as a desperate grasp from a grief-stricken loved one for a sign from the universe, the reports of butterflies were not just mine. All members of our family individually reported the sudden influx. Friends reported them. My parents' home, our bunker of grief, was swamped with majestic Monarch butterflies. And so I gripped tightly to this symbol.

The chrysalis is the container of transformation where the caterpillar enters and the butterfly exits. It is a tale of destruction and a tale of hope, where destruction via digestion of the old is overshadowed by the potentiality of the beautiful new.

\* \* \*

## *Bucketing the deluge*

*Bucketing the deluge*
*in desperate striving*
*to keep afloat.*
*Depths of soul*
*shrouded in darkness*
*demand life,*
*demand to be met*
*in waking*
*existence.*
*Closing doors,*
*the usual path*
*to run from the pitter-patter*
*of dark reign*
*that cries out in the night*
*Delaying the sobriety,*
*a jester's call*
*mocks the inevitability*
*of failure.*
*Hasty decisions*
*lead to dark paths*
*with gloomy corners.*
*Till the moment*
*relatedness shows up.*
*Wild, so wild*
*threatening to buck this youngling*
*with its ferocity.*

*Tempering this temper*
*as a dance through the mud.*
*Sticky footprints grip the body*
*under the weight of struggle.*
*Till the wild*
*meets the domestic*
*and wisdom*
*transmutes.*

Personally, Kev's death began the chrysalis formation. The energetic fury of tragedy catapulted me out of my sleep state. The pain provided contrast and a deep knowing that I would never be the same again.

I had crossed a threshold of no return.

An Initiation had begun.

Initiation comes from the Latin word **"*initium*"** which means to begin. Throughout our lives, we cross a litany of thresholds. Thresholds of no return begin with initiation, where the line crossed is erased when we first step foot on the other side. There's no turning back. This abduction across the threshold left me dazed and confused. As the descent into darkness began, I fumbled my way through it. What to do without him? The fumblings began with mimicry. Our desire to fit in is hardwired into our biology to help us survive. French Philosopher Rene Girard's Mimetic Theory of Desire proposes that we use imitation to survive and learn. Being the '*interdividual*', not the individual allows us to find strength in numbers. And I needed this collective strength to survive.

Being a shy kid and the eldest meant that mimicry was my default mode. Shapeshifting constantly just to fade into the background was a skill I had perfected. And so when I felt myself fighting for my life, I defaulted to tools I knew best. I observed others who seemed to have meaning, purpose, happiness in their lives and I copied. Initially, it provided a welcome distraction. A drug high to escape to. But there was always the inevitable come down. Gasping for some semblance of meaning and light, I reached for quick fixes that gave meaning to the charade. But each and every time, I'd only end up more lost.

\* \* \*

### *Con Form*

*I con form.*
*Pied Piper emulation*
*swaying*
*to dismay*
*in dis-guise.*
*Shapeshifting on repeat,*
*the original worn bare thin.*
*Scattered and tattered,*
*the inner volume*

*crackles with feedback.*
*What am I if I am you?*
*Am I but an imprint*
*or clone*
*or delightfully original in genesis?*
*I can't know.*
*I don't know.*
*I've forgotten.*
*I con form.*
*I conform.*

The mimicry only amplified the struggle I'd always had with self-worth. External validation was a way of fitting in, especially for a shy kid. During my twenties, that was achieved by being the life of the party whilst under the influence. Inebriated, my persona was pleasing to others and this validation was enough to keep the self-worth demons at bay. I was fun to be around. A happy drunk who always wore a smile. Which was for the most part, genuine. Alcohol allowed surrender. Hidden aspects of my personality came out to play and I enjoyed the freedom of being seen. Or so I thought. I didn't know any different. Prior to Kev's death, I lived solely for the weekend.

Party.
Recover.
Tick boxes at work.
Rinse Repeat.

After Kev, a night out was hollow. A bottomless void I tried to fill with more alcohol. More drugs. More of anything to numb me. The numbness provided time travel to a world before the descent. But it was temporary and I could feel my feet slipping on that terrain. The angle of descent beckoning me forward, whispering in my ear to surrender.

*"The bottom awaits."*
*"The bottom awaits."*

\* \* \*

### *Scorched Scars*

*On the crest of forgetting*
*lies the scorched scars*
*of the knowing.*
*A hollow whisper*
*on the winds*
*waiting for the forest*
*of ears to open.*
*The amnesia;*
*begins the initiation*
*into nature.*
*Beckoning the youngling forward.*
*With each step to the side,*

*we are called back.*
*Called to honour the fact*
*that we are made,*
*not born*
*So step toward*
*genesis.*

Yearning for an elixir to quench my thirsty soul, I found little nourishment in the shiniest trinkets. To the outside world, my life post-Kev's death was professionally and personally successful. I worked through the mimic to-do list of what a successful life was, with validation and accolades piling up.

So many summits. So much absence. Life's accelerator flat to the floor with a fervour that knew no bounds. But I wasn't at the wheel. I was a mere passenger. A passenger in a life spent collecting presents without presence. A hungry ghost.

\* \* \*

## *Where do you go?*

*Where do you go?*
*Craned curvature the donned flesh,*
*a cardboard cut out*
*complete with disinterest and disdain.*
*Empty minutes pile up*

*lost to the saccharine;*
*the quick fix of a thirsty mind.*
*Chasing the short tail of bliss,*
*ravaging the territory*
*for the golden ticket*
*when the prize*
*lies in the youthful breath*
*of a shirt-tugging monkey.*
*The mirror of time travel*
*exposes only*
*a deathbed of regret*
*and wasted minutes.*
*Where do you go*
*when you're here?*

My descent into the valley of darkness picked up speed with more to-do list accolades and the hollow yearnings I screamed towards. The veneer of success, the picket fence house, the dream job, amazing wife, two beautiful kids, all were fracturing before my eyes. A mere observer of my life. Not a participant. And I was fast running out of fingers to plug the leaks in the crucible.

But in the crucible of grief, amongst the dross, sadness is not the only one present.

The beginnings of a conversation with death hold magic. Through the magic of reminiscence, laughter and smiles find their way into our souls as old stories help savour the reverence of moments.

The warm embrace of a surrendered hug. The breath we took for granted, honoured for its sacredness. The remembering of the fragility of life. The latency of potential that lies in every moment if we choose to live into it. The dreams once held at a distance, now alive with new meaning. The new beginnings and growth.

The unfortunate part was that I chose to only see the world one way. The lies I told myself only served to further agitate. A deep gnawing that I was not living truthfully. I was playing the victim. In conversation, it would only be a matter of seconds before I introduced my brother's death.

> ***"Look at poor me, I've lived through tragedy."***

I wore my perpetual state of mourning as a badge of honour. I relived his death every day and died every day to the past. A past I couldn't change. A past I couldn't impact.

In his story, I saw only tragedy.

I saw only missed birthdays. Missed family events. Missed milestones. And these for sure are tragic...but I was missing half the story.

*"The issue is not simply the question of life or death; the real issue is not being fully alive, for that is also a kind of death."*

*MICHAEL MEADE - AWAKENING THE SOUL*

\* \* \*

## *Barbs of Deceit*

*Caught on thorny brambles of lies,*
*truth lacerates,*
*bleeding out*
*onto soil*
*in despair.*
*Movement is stagnant,*
*snagged on barbs*
*of deceit.*
*Why do these words escape*
*to cover tracks*
*of wrongful imprints?*
*Why shy from the breath of honesty?*
*Whose refreshment*
*allow jaws*
*to unclench.*
*Truth.*
*Fully.*
*Truth.*

*Truthfully.
I don't know,
but that would be
a lie.*

# 4

# Dark Dawns

The night is darkest before dawn.

British Theologian Thomas Fuller calls it the *'dark night of the soul.'* That dark night met daylight, with another ferocious argument with my wife in front of our kids. We spurted divorceful venom at each other. Two souls in love since our eyes first met were as far apart as ever. My kids cried as their parents unhinged. I left the house screaming. Running away, as usual, I slammed the door in anger.

Then an intervention took place.

Fumbling, I dropped my keys. Blood boiling in my veins, I picked the keys up to close the door. As I did, the violence in my body was met with the magic of a moment. With my left hand still on the key in the door, a beautiful Monarch butterfly with striking orange patterns landed on my right shoulder.

……Frozen I stood.

My hand…still on the key. Staring in stillness at each other for what felt like an eternity, I felt a deep knowing come over me. The butterfly, his hand on my shoulder.

> *"Hush, hush dear brother."*
> *"It's time."*

\* \* \*

## Whisperings

*I scream at you in whispers.*
*WAKE UP!*
*But stratus clouds*
*hang you up and out,*
*a weathering of scalding tumult.*
*From vantages within reach,*
*I plead with you*
*to ride*
*the ephemeral out.*

*Impermanence is...the only permanence.*
*Catch an inhale.*
*Ride an exhale*
*with freedom for*
*the only truth*
*is always waiting.*
*Always here.*

Most days, I ran to punish myself. Running while listening to our shared love of punk rock music was how I coped. To shift the pain. It was the only way to survive the storm. Straight after my Monarch moment, I set off on my run listening to a playlist of his favourite songs.

The clouds covered my landscape with a storm of tears while Anberlin and Rise Against sang our favourites in my ear. It wasn't unusual for me to try and outrun the pain. But this time was different. On this day I stopped running away from the storm. Instead, I ran straight towards the eye of it.

\* \* \*

## *Become your storm*

*Become your storm*
*with deep surrender*
*to booming thunder*

*and the lightning
of wildness.
To fight as flight
the sheer tenacity
of resistance
leaves our boats
weathered,
anchored,
stranded.
Become your storm
with deep fervour,
dying into winds of discontent
with heartfelt joy.
Awaken to the aliveness
of being broken
on rocks
for alive
is a life alight
with the radiance
of a moment.
Become your storm!*

Out the other side, I finished the run, and there it was. A lightness I'd not felt for a very long time. Morning had arrived in the valley of my soul. The dark night passed. And once again I heard the call.

A haptic reminder that life works in mysterious ways. Perhaps not so much out of the blue, but out of the black, it was my dear friend Bec with an offer to keynote a conference. With a face of dry tears, I pressed questions. When? Where? What time? As the answers landed in my ears, there was that familiar feeling again.

The date would be the tenth anniversary.

The tenth anniversary of hearing the words

"Kev's dead."

It was then I knew that the healing would only begin with surrender to the quest. And the price of admission on this quest was nothing short of everything.

Death, the price of admission.

So I paid in story.

His/story.

\* \* \*

## *Hand scribbled maps*

*The road less traveled*
*with its hand-scribbled maps*

*of just around the corner*
*drives my soul.*
*With curious steps*
*and an open heart,*
*I walk with quest*
*on my mind*
*and in my bones.*
*A litany of thresholds*
*complete with drowning descents*
*digests the form*
*that I seek to shed.*
*I grip, it rips*
*for fear all order will be lost.*
*Swallowed in the soup of chaos,*
*I find the magic in the tension*
*Tumbling with half bodies*
*into the darkness,*
*I seek to see eye to eye*
*with completion.*
*Searching for wholeness*
*in the hole*
*that eats me up.*
*Tender hooks my only prop,*
*for standing up*
*and in*
*the grief that gripped*
*for so long.*

Sharing his story in such a public forum was the first real transmission to my world that I was not ok. To a sea of friends, colleagues, and strangers, I spoke to the impact. A cry for help was heard. Heard in the similar stories we all carry as wounded warriors of life but are too afraid to share. In the mirror of the collective, the water stilled long enough for me to catch a glimpse. A glimpse of the state of me.

His story was not my story. It did not define me. But I felt called to share. To share as an offering. To share is an offering, to help light the inner flame we all carry in our hearts.

Staring into the still water revealed to me that I had been lighting the wrong fire.

\* \* \*

## *Danger*

*What if I am the danger?*
*The dream killer*
*The fire starter*
*The slayer of hope*
*How do I confront the shadow*
*that drowns and douses*
*in vernacular*
*when all seems well*

*on the surface*
*This Prodigal son*
*holds me dearly*
*in chains*
*and love*
*I'm sorry*
*I threw you to the curb*
*A discard*
*of fumbled ways*
*So I welcome with radiance*
*and reverence*
*the spirit*
*of your endeavour*
*The war is over.*

Death is not a comfortable topic for most. A type of social leprosy where when the container is opened, people backtrack with apologies and awkward scrambles. *"Please, anywhere but here."*

When the pain is too raw, threatening to swallow you in clouded darkness, everyone asks how you are doing. But radio silence when you are finally ready to speak.

It's not their fault. Life keeps on moving but grief is trauma and trauma has steep demands to be met and moved through. Trauma release is a necessity that needs to be spoken alive.

And as a society, we need to get better at holding space for the deep catharsis required when picking up the pieces. The holding of such space is the deepest love you can give a person. The space to cry into the void left by love's absence.

To speak alive and release the trauma.

# 5

# Perturbation

*"To stay with that shakiness - to stay with a broken heart, with a rumbling stomach, with the feeling of hopelessness and wanting to get revenge - that is the path of true awakening. Sticking with that uncertainty, getting the knack of relaxing in the midst of chaos, learning not to panic - this is the spiritual path."*

**PEMA CHODRON - WHEN THINGS FALL APART**

I remember when I finally let out the screams that kept me awake at night. Once again, I was speaking alive his/story. It was the final presentation of an eight-week public speaking masterclass. Held in a beautiful container by Clare Dea, I journeyed through the world of improvisation, deep presencing, and authentic expression. The masterclass culminated in a live performance in front of family and friends. My story was about the wrestle I have with the many masks I wear in life.

A wrestle amplified by grief and constant shapeshifting.

Speaking about the pain in front of strangers is difficult but doing so in front of your parents and siblings trumps that. The presentation was edgy for me, requiring deep authenticity and complete surrender. Every time I reached the threshold's edge, I'd back away. So deeply afraid of what was beyond the line I had marked in the sand, I continually pulled out during practice.

The edginess of finally letting go scared me to death.

But speaking the pain alive while I looked into the eyes of my Mum, Dad and sister Linda tipped me over the edge. The pain of the last few years erupted in a scream that shook the room to its core. The silence was the silence I'd been craving since the day he left. The spontaneous eruption was the moment of deep surrender where I met the pain and released that to the world. When that scream left me, I dropped into a moment of deep union with the universe. All the masks fell away. There was no 'I' giving a performance. We were one.

A oneness I had rarely felt since that call. It is only now I can conceptually understand what pushed me over that edge.

Unbeknownst to me, each practice had charged my emotional cup. Filling my crucible to the brim with concentrated energy. Seeing my reflection in the tears on my parent's cheeks was the final charge, the principle of Perturbation took over, guiding me over the threshold. Thank you Buckminster Fuller and Christine McDougall for the retrospective sight to understand what happened that night.

I found safety in the container created by Clare and my fellow participants and I charged the transformation with a rich vein of ongoing energy. The scream was a release of deep trauma and allowed me to cross the threshold of transformation.

A wave of deep flow carried me forward.

And so began, the ascent.

\* \* \*

## Spontaneous Eruptions

*Oh what magic births from souls holding court*
*with love.*
*Where depths of whispers are weaved into song,*
*spoken alive with listening.*

*Like water traversing the contours of land,*
*we spontaneously erupt the never before.*
*The magic of maybe dancing with the edges,*
*knocking on new world doorways*
*as adjacent possibilities are dreamt into existence.*
*I die in those moments of presence.*
*Katana cut narratives*
*fall away in reverent shards*
*as the sacred beingness*
*is witnessed.*
*Singing hearts heard by*
*tractor beam connection.*
*There is no separation,*
*only love.*
*Divine love,*
*swallowing you in the deepest embrace.*
*Gifted,*
*I sit back with a face full of smile.*
*Oh the places we will go*
*with love in our hearts.*

# 2

# Albedo - The Whitening

---

*"The search is over when you realize that the true and lasting fulfillment you have been searching for is found to be nowhere other than right where you are. It is here. It is in you, it is in me, it is in all life, both sentient and insentient. It is everywhere."*

---

**GANGAJI - DIAMOND IN YOUR POCKET**

# 6

# The Ascent

Although the first steps were shaky, the days following were blissful. I felt the shackles of the dark grief that held me back for so long, loosen. Fuelled by a glimpse of oneness, a light in the lament, I yearned to sprint. The union, a new peak to scale. A gasp of hope I desperately wanted to get back to. But the deliberate act of seeking often left me pathless and confused. The high. The bliss. The surrender. How could I get back there? The old patterns of seeking, seeking quick remedies.

\* \* \*

## *In this*

*But in this,*
*is it.*
*The very thing*
*but not, a thing.*
*The greatest gift*
*but not, a gift*
*to have, to hold.*
*The it*
*cannot be named,*
*for anchors have no grip,*
*is it all*
*and nothing at once.*
*So be in this,*
*for this*
*is*
*isness.*

I learned that the mystery cannot be trapped. The ineffable cannot be named, tamed, or gamed. Surrender through deep flow states provides nothing but a glimpse. A temporary remembering of the forgotten. An escape from the mental minutiae we constantly treadmill to.

The old game of doing will not do.

Any attempt to corral, to control, leaves you stuck in the

quicksand of old patterns and behaviours. I was switching blackness of grief for lightness of bliss. But they were one and the same. Chasing bliss is bypassing. A bypass of the work, where the real healing happens. Both are needed. As Buckminster Fuller would say, Unity is Plural at minimum two.

*High and low.*
*Spirit and soul.*
*Death and birth.*
*Love and hurt.*

The collapse into oneness, the ultimate.
A union.
A return home.

\* \* \*

### Icarus

*I trust in the medicine*
*to hold these wings of Icarus in place.*
*Clouds wrap these fingers*
*with a glimpse of the macrocosm.*
*Soaring till scorched edges*
*fail to hear screams of wise words*
*Remember!*
*Remember the remembering.*

*The laws of the one verse
masked by glimpses of heaven
hollowing form before time,
until I stray too far.
Yearning falters.
Learned landing prevents burn up
on re-entry.
Prevents dis-integration.*

> "Be sceptical of the quick route. It's truly what's got us
> into a thousand unruly messes. And not the kind the
> poets praise."

**MARTIN SHAW - COURTING THE WILD TWIN**

The path to healing is slow. Anyone who tells otherwise is bullshitting you. Through growth, we allow our wounds to heal. The healing, works to a natural rhythm of ebbs and flows, charting a beautiful non-linear path. Only the ego tries to hurry nature along. And that egoic movement causes the knitting of fresh wounds to split. And we fall backward, ruptured again. Be prepared for stumbles and backward steps. Be prepared for the stories of past and future to adorn your inner movie screen. Incessant mind itches that promise to crawl in uninvited and steal moments.

\* \* \*

## *Itchy*

*The mind is itchy again.*
*Projected scratchings*
*filled to the brim*
*with loathing.*
*Hmm...*
*How to care for beastly angels*
*that caress with one hand*
*and stab with the other?*
*Origination rising*
*from heart to mind*
*rapid.*
*No room for breath*
*as sleight of hand*
*distracts with distraction.*
*Oh...to claw at this skin*
*as if it were real*
*and beg for reprieve.*
*But*
*If I can't find the mind.*
*From where comes the itch?*

The ebb and flow of progress humbled me, teaching me to sit in my own life. To live into the moments that were gifted to me every day. Presence is an art form. A dying art form. The only thing we ever truly have is this gift we give ourselves and others. The gift of the moment. Being present, my progressive steps helped sure my footing. Being held in space began the repair of relationships. An emerging awareness of how disembodied I had been. So presence helped begin the relating. The relating to each moment and bearing witness to the magical details in every interaction. Hiding always in plain sight, a mysterious miracle welcomed with open eyes, ears, and hearts.

Life.

\* \* \*

## *Witnessing*

*Rock trophies collected by vagabonds*
*with dirty shoes and brazen hearts*
*saunter with crane kicks and near fall ins.*
*Dogs off-leash terrorise with abandon*
*as rivers of ever flow fold-over crags and crests.*
*Bon voyage as flower boats of the young set sail*
*with winded smiles.*
*Hidden in the shadow's, man's doing.*
*Artefacts of snagged indulgence,*
*evidence of fractured relationships.*
*Nature's Prodigal son,*
*lost in the mind-field*
*of ego*

*and mine.*
*Colour strewn across this magnificent canvas*
*by youthful exuberance,*
*proof the arms of natus*
*are wide open*
*and ready for embrace.*
*Always.*

# 7

# Relatedness

Death's impact woke me up with a bang, leaving a deep cavern in my heart. It is only now that I deeply cherish that moment. Those scars, still raw. But the pain taught me just how ferociously I love. Grief's impact is loss and love. They are polarities that need each other to exist. Unity is plural at a minimum of two.

I love deeply. I grieve deeply.

And there is no other way I would choose to live.

Relatedness, is how Martin Shaw says we wake up. More than just our relationships between humans, it is how we relate to all nature. How we are woven into the fabric of all life. Death changed the way I relate. I awoke to the fragility of life. To the rawness that transpires in every moment. To the savage reality, rapturous beauty, and potent subtleties present in every moment. I rediscovered how to be in *"religio"* or deep communion with the universe. In deep communion with my own signs of nature. In the deepest of communion with my own Signature Sound.

\* \* \*

## *Signature Sound*

*What do you sound like when you finally speak?*

*Swallowed keys to
padlocks
of your own doing
succumb to surrender
and crossed lines.
Words from depths
of the otherworld
gasp through lips,
finally free,
finally me.
Signature sounds
of tone embodied
in story filled with
eros and amor.*

*Soulful flows fill
high to low
in decadent
traipsing
across barren lands.
Finally,
nourishment
drowns the soil of
fractured grounding.*

*We've been waiting.
We've been waiting.*

*The ground now sure,
embraces the first
imprint of you.*

*What do you sound like when you finally speak?*

The ascent began a continuous series of threshold crossings. Guided by constants in my dreams, where clearings met dark forests, I could feel the pull of the unknown. I'd dance at the edge before I'd cross. This required deep surrender, trust, and a knowing that this was the path. It was here that the phrase *"walk-on"* became a powerful ally. Kev lived and died on the other side of his thresholds. As a 17-year-old, he had moved to the United States in the hope of playing NCAA College Basketball. Attending a High School in Savannah, Georgia as a Junior, Kev would take the team all the way to the State Championships. Averaging 28.4 points per game and setting a single-season record for assists, Kev's star was on the rise.

And then it wasn't.

Forced to sit out his Senior year, hopes of a Division 1 scholarship faded fast. His toes once again graced the threshold. The dream fraying at the edges. These crossings demand everything from us. A complete death. And this is deeply scary. To help us hold our nerve, we need the counsel of wise elders. Souls that see us for who we are and provide the stability to target our energy toward traverse. For Kev, this was his American Dad, Mark Sussman. Suss, as he is affectionately known, hustled and hustled to give Kev every opportunity of achieving his dream. Empowering purpose, by giving Kev the coaching gig for the Junior Varsity team during his season of ineligibility. Kev responded by showing up to every game in his best suit. His only suit. When life knocks us down, we need to rise up with a smile on our face looking our dashing best.

He practiced like he was still playing. Because he was. Every. Day.

He did the work. Every. Day.

Suss's hustle landed Kev two opportunities. One was a full ride (scholarship) to a Division II school. He would start as a freshman and be guaranteed plenty of court time. The second, to attend Georgia as a student and be a *"walk-on"* player. Part bench warmer, part cheerleader. No guarantees.

So now instead of a threshold to cross, Kev was presented with a crossroads.

The safe bet versus the long shot.

*Have you been here before?*

For Kev, it was a no-brainer. Georgia all the way. He called Dad and told him he would rather live knowing that he went for it than to take the safe bet. The threshold beckoned. To attend Georgia, Kev needed to get the required grades. Schoolwork was not his forte. But he did the work, got the grades, and found himself at Georgia on his own academic merits.

Threshold crossed.

He became a walk-on player for the University of Georgia.

Threshold crossed.

His performances in his first year led to the offer. A full scholarship.

Threshold crossed.

> "A master who was once asked, What is the Tao—the Way? replied, Walk on. Actually, Go! As we say, Go, man! Go! Go, go. To be stopped at a certain point is what is called 'having a doubt,' as when one fumbles, or wobbles, or hesitates about something—trying to find the right solution for the circumstances by thinking it out in a situation where there really is no time to think it out."

*ALAN WATTS - OUT OF OUR MIND*

Just go. Walk on. Go! Go! Go! Kev's unwavering dedication to walking on in life became a powerful catalyst for my growth and healing. And like him, I needed the counsel of wise teachers, elders, and souls to help with my wobbles at the threshold's edge.

I was blessed with so many...

My wife
My family.
Mentors
Medicine men and women.
Experiential learning.
Nature
Plants.
Knowledge.

*Forgetting knowledge.*
Sisterhood.
Brotherhood.
Community.

Slowly but surely, my eyes began to open. On the other side of the threshold, beauty let the light in. Flowers burst through the charred remains, signalling new life. New beginnings that honoured the death of before, compost for growth and nourishment. That new growth needed tending, with dialogue the nourishment that helped hold the alchemy. Helped lead become gold.

Speaking alive story is an energetic transmission that requires the deepest trust of friends and welcome ears. Friendship was the altar where I prayed. With conversation, I felt held. I felt new and nourished. Conversation was alchemical, especially when it was with my Anam Caras.

Anam Cara is Gaelic for *"soul friend."* Friendship beyond interest and time. Friendships where time is lost to the magic of moments. People who see you beyond the barriers you put up for protection. A friendship where your nature is naked and witnessed.

To those who I have sat across tables from, my soul thanks you for saving me.

Thanks you for seeing me. Thanks you for your kind, hard

words. Thanks you for the banter of timeless conversation that heal as words leave lips. Thanks you for the ears of welcome.

> *"With the anam cara you could share your innermost self, your mind, and your heart. This friendship was an act of recognition and belonging. When you had an anam cara, your friendship cut across all convention, morality, and category. You were joined in an ancient and eternal way with the "friend of your soul."*

*JOHN O' DONAHOE - ANAM CARA*

\* \* \*

## *Anam Cara*

*To be seen is to be born.*
*Born again in erupted splendour,*
*held in the gaze of those*
*who wade past the thorny brambles you've planted,*
*to the hiding place where your soul*
*is singing the song you were born to sing.*
*Rapturous conversations engulf you.*
*Emergent possibilities tumble into notes and hand gestures*
*as the mystical arrives.*
*Ancient songs spilling from old souls*
*who've sat across tables before,*

*ignite conversations that will be remembered
in old ears on deathbeds.
Life gifts you only so many of these encounters.
Spaces where the never shared
flows with sovereignty and surrender.
Places where your fierce wildness lives in each breath.
The Emerald Isle in me
knows the deep words that capture the magic of this relatedness.*

*Anam Cara
Soul friend*

*Stories are alive in the moments carved by anam caras.
Deep listening, synchronicity,
co-created sentences, 'yes and' spontaneity.
Rabbit holes and faraway lands.
Another round of green tea and long black please,
our souls have catching up to do.*

# 8

# Union

*"Only people who are capable of loving strongly can also suffer great sorrow, but this same necessity of loving serves to counteract their grief and heals them."*

**LEO TOLSTOY - CHILDHOOD, BOYHOOD, YOUTH**

Among healers, there is a saying, *"you have to feel it to heal it."* Feeling the hurt and not running from the pain is deep soul work. Soul work that drives us deep into the underworld of our own psyche. Feeling this healing extends deep roots which provide anchor for the rise of our spirit. Like bamboo, the magical healing takes place underground. Invisible to the outside world. But it enables and empowers the shoots to reach with majesty to the sky. My healing, nourished by daily commitments to be in relationship with life. Micro practices led to transformations of the macro variety. Expression through music, prose, and weaving the two. Space through meditation, solo time, and inquiry. Nourishment through movement, sleep, and nutrition. Over time, my roots took hold. I started to reconnect with enchantment. Conformity, sheepwalking, and mimicry fell away. The simple things cleared the lines for signal transmission. Helped me wake up to the yearning of songs I was born to sing.

My song of enchantment.

Within each of us is, as David Whyte animates beautifully, *"one line already written."* The line that you contribute to the story of the world.

This can only be heard in place.

In situ.

\* \* \*

### *In situ*

*In situ.*
*Your original place,*
*the nested crevice*
*where inception birthed*

*the roots that explode*
*from seed of genius.*
*Genesis from genes*
*of perfect oneness*
*firmly in place.*
*Rested in situ.*

When I looked forward on my path, I saw a deep mist covering the landscape. Looking back over my shoulder helped provide clues. The origin of the word *'clue'*, Michael Meade writes in The Genius Myth, is from the Saxon word 'clew.' It means a ball of thread. Pulling on that ball of thread revealed the way back home to my own story. It highlighted moments of aliveness where I got out of my own way. It highlighted shadows that I ran from. It highlighted work that I needed to feel to heal. Yet, the biggest clue of all...

A threshold crossing that I was too young to hold.

My life began where blood, oppression, and spirit are woven into the soil. The countryside of Garranstackle, Bree in County Wexford, Ireland held me for nine beautiful years. The adventures of a dreamer wove in between fields of strawberries, fields my Uncles tended to, and the spirit of a culture that will never stop singing. Even when the world threatens to quash them.

Arriving in the land of ancient wisdom that is Australia, I

felt lost. With no clue that I was lost. I had crossed a threshold to get there. I remember clearly holding Kev's hand as we walked on the tarmac of Shannon Airport. I remember my parents crying, looking back over their shoulders to the windows where the tears of our family fogged the glass. My roots, transplanted from Emerald to Sunburst lands. Australia welcomed me with open arms. But it was a Western welcome. The feeling of being displaced never left. I had tucked that feeling away deep inside. And it kept calling. For place matters.

How we relate, how we commune, how we honour.

All need to be grounded in place.

My final step toward union was to truly meet the land I'd cried blood spilled tears into.

\* \* \*

## *Stormy eyes*

*Die into the eye of the storm,*
*laughing tears of deep surrendering death.*
*Lash me with the truth of what is,*
*for I come bearing gifts.*
*Sovereign humble choices*
*of a man*

*standing with two feet firm.*
*Wither with weather,*
*scars of destructive creation.*
*Find home on this skin,*
*cutting to bone,*
*rememories.*
*Here I stand with open arms,*
*crying into the sun*
*that lights the way.*
*Held in holds of men,*
*who lean into the spaces I traverse.*
*For now, the fire clears,*
*the old way;*
*making way for growth*
*on blackened edges.*
*Char crumbles breaking underfoot*
*as brave new paths appear.*
*Ashes rising in mythical meanderings*
*and power quests.*

*..............................................*

*Breathe deep dear brother*
*You're held in stead*
*by the weight of your wait.*
*But the time has come.*

My nature yearned for nature. So with permission, I quested. An ancient way of meeting the land that holds us, questing quietens the chatter and busyness of human doing through subtraction. Sitting in a three-metre by three-metre space in the middle of the Australian bush, I subtracted.

Food.

Vices.

Distraction.

Busyness.

Alone but not lonely, I stood still long enough to be in *'dialogos'* with the land. Stripped of everything, I was naked to life. The shadows that I feared to meet head-on appeared before me. This was the work.

And the land went to work on me.

Noises in the black of night.
Snakes.
Dirt in every orifice.
The skin ripped as I shed it.

Nature met nature.

> "We have to shift our attitude of ownership of nature to relationship with nature. The moment you change from ownership to relationship, you create a sense of the sacred."
>
> **SATISH KUMAR**

Changed, I emerged. With a language, I never knew I possessed. Poetry. Before that time, I had written only a handful of poems. But the language of the exiled built the bridge between my worlds. Moments written alive with a reverie that causes my heart to skip a beat. Words that honour the bardic tradition of my homeland and the songlines of the sunburst country I call home.

For the first time since Kev passed, I was at peace. Peace in the knowing that life is circular, temporary in this form, but alight in each moment.

Alive.
A life alight in the radiance of a moment.

# 3

# Rubedo - The Reddening

"When it's over, I want to say: all my life
I was a bride married to amazement.
I was the bridgeroom,
taking the world into my arms."

**MARY OLIVER - "WHEN DEATH COMES" FROM
NEW AND SELECTED POEMS**

## 9

# Love's Fire

It has taken fifteen years for these words to be spoken through me. I know Kev helped spur them on. I've wrestled with the ebbs and flows of speaking alive the pain. Often feeling like it would engulf me in flames. But I can't say it enough...

*"The feeling is the healing."*

Life is alive, yet only if we choose to live into each moment. The depth of love we carry in our hearts comes packaged with grief. Lament is a fiery tribute to the ferocity of our love.

And for me, a light on the path ahead.
The mist has lifted.

\* \* \*

## *An ode to lament*

*I am alight in the lament.*
*Screaming in fire*
*as the flames of mourning*
*burn the superfluous.*
*Cinders.*
*Embers.*
*A light.*
*A light in the lament.*
*I am alive in the flames,*
*not regretting lost moments*
*for I am alive in the remembering*
*that I love this deeply.*
*And the depths provide all the guidance I need,*
*for I love with a ferocity that burns me alive.*
*Alive is lament's song.*
*A song we are all born to sing.*

To you dear reader, I lay my heart bare. The rawness of this transmission wasn't easy to write. No life is lived without suffering. We were born through a portal of distress. Our beautiful mothers laboured to carry us in their wombs and breathe life into us through birth. The rawness is a call to honour the unique expression of our own being. Life is not the pursuit of more. Those who have reached those peaks know their faulty promises. To live means to continue.

*To remain.*

For those who have lost loved ones, living after loss is difficult to continue. Difficult to remain. But we know that the loves of our lives remain with us. Since Kev left and sent back butterflies, my family has grown. My community has grown. Grown to share in the love we have for Kev. His legacy is seen in the spirit of new birth. Seen in the spirit of his friends now being my dear friends. Seen in the spirit that lives and breathes in me.

He will never be in my rearview, for I carry his love with me in my heart. Walking with me. Walking with each of the people whose lives he touched.

To grief, I say thank you. Thank you for showing how deeply humans love. The void is not loss but the magnitude of magic another human being gifts to us. And there is no other way to live.

Kev, I finally finished it mate. Thank you. I love you.

# 10

# Bibliography

The following works have helped inspire, shape and sharpen my own Signature Sound. I am deeply grateful for the wisdom within the prose.

Alan Watts - *Out of Your Mind*
Amy Edmondson - *A Fuller Explanation*
Bill Plotkin - *Soulcraft*
Buckminster Fuller - *Critical Path*
Christine McDougall - *Blog: Beauty of Beginnings*
Christine McDougall - *Syntropic World Masterclass*
David Whyte - *House of Belonging*
Dennis William Hauck - *The Emerald Tablet*
Gangaji - *Diamond in your Pocket*
Jamie Wheal - *Recapture the Rapture*

Jamie Wheal & Steven Kotler - *Stealing Fire*

Jeremy Lent - *The Alchemy of Heartbreak and Hope: A Spiritual Practice for Our Time*

John O'Donohue - *Anam Cara*

Leo Tolstoy - *Childhood, Boyhood, Youth*

Martin Shaw - *Courting The Wild Twin*

Mary Oliver - *New and Selected Poems*

Michael Meade - *Awakening the Soul*

Michael Meade - *The Genius Myth*

Pema Chodron - *When Things Fall Apart*

Satish Kumar - *Spiritual Ecology*

Wolfgang Palaver - *René Girard's Mimetic Theory*

# 11

# Acknowledgments

The space where I most likely forget someone. I am so blessed to have such amazing human beings in my community. To those, I have forgotten, know that you are in my heart.

* * *

Benny Wallington and Leslie Lau - I am forever grateful for the love, guidance, editing prowess, and willingness to hold me steady during the birthing process of this book. You helped me find my Signature Sound and I look forward to our Signature Sound Community growing. My deepest gratitude brothers.

Ollie, brother, Daisy dude...thank you for taking the time to read and share your heartfelt responses on our walks. The shape of this book is greater as a result.

Jiro Taylor - What can I say to a man who has helped me wade through the darkest period of my life. You have been the light for me for the last five years. Your counsel, wisdom, and zest for life have been oxygen for my soul. Thank you from the bottom of my heart.

Shambhala Warrior Brothers - This book does not exist without you. Sitting in circle with brothers who bravely stand up in their own lives has been a well that has enriched my week, my year, my life. Honoured to be in your presence.

Leon Cossar - Your bardic soul gifted me the language that adorns these pages. Story. Myth. Poetry. Thank you for the remembering.

The Fellowship - Gents, tis an honour to walk a year and a day alongside you.

The Signature Sound Community - Dooz, Dan, Richard, Chris, Willy, Rob - getting to listen to your Signature Sound every week is a blessing. I look forward to your song meeting the world.

Lara Foster - One of my favourite humans. Thank you for helping co-create Hedge School. Your enthusiasm for life has kept a fire lit in me.

The Hedge School community - Who knew the simple power of posting weekly from the heart would lead to a small little community of beautiful souls. Thank you for reading each week.

Oceania Regen Network (OcRe) - Bob, Benny, Maxx...what a crew a joyful sailors! Earth healing all the way.

My School family - I'm blessed to work with such inspiring people every day.

Jamie Wheal and the Flow Genome Project Community - Flow brought me to you. Catharsis and Community brought me home with my eyes and heart wide open. Thank you!

My Kokoro Boat Team - Georgia Ellis, Takako Hoshi, Benny Wallington, Rob Gronbeck, Damon Valentino, Clare Sarah Johnson, Sarah Sarkis, and Cara Bradley - From our first conversations about Death over Dinner, I knew our weave together would be special. Such an amazing group of human beings.

Christine McDougall, Murray Galbraith and the Syntropic World Community - I am blessed to find myself in a community whose purpose is to build a better world for everyone. Christine, your poetic soul speaks so clearly to mine. Thank you for the guidance.

Clare Dea - Thank you dear sister for creating a container that caused the storyteller in me to finally birth. To my dear friends who danced with me during those eight weeks, thank you for seeing me.

Deb Sukarna - I have learned so much about leadership and life from you. You are a truly marvelous human being.

Michael Lauria - Brother, you are an inspiration. Thank you for our always beautiful dialogues and your wisdom on self-publishing.

Steve Glaveski - Heavy music, creating art, and asking deep questions weave us together and I thank you for the inspiration and wisdom along the way.

Tom Barrett - A coach of the highest calibre. Our conversations have helped me be a better human being.

Kristina Garla - Long blacks, green teas, and so many anam cara conversations. This book is because of you and our conversational alchemy.

Caiyuda Kiora & Colin Hawkshaw - You both are medicina of the highest ilk.

Kynan, Michelle, Kalani Robinson, and the Enrusk team - I cannot thank you enough for helping bring Kev's story to life. Words aren't enough to capture my gratitude.

Bec Spink - Thank you for the Universal sign and the faith to speak. A true catalyst for the birth of this book.

Pachamama - Life is animate in everything I see and cannot see. Thank you for holding the tears of heartbreak and holding Kev in his final resting place, in your arms.

Mark, Maxine, Jill, and Brian Sussman - Kev's American family. What can we say but the boy sure knew how to land on his feet. Thank you for loving him as your own. He most certainly loved you guys!

Dave Bliss - Big Dawg, thank you for being his co-conspirator of mischief and our giant friend. We are forever entwined. Kev's American brothers - Jeff Smith, Josh Smith, Matt Hunt, Davy Clay - You were all meant to meet and he loved you deeply. Thank you from one brother to another. So much mischief, so many laughs, so many tears. Deeply honoured to call you my brothers.

Kev's American family - it sure does take a village. Thank you Savannah and UGA. The Hunt family, Jacob Rauer, Mollie Ramage Wiese, Dennis and Melanie Felton, Pete and Sharon Herrmann, Kate and Joel Bliss the list goes on. Sorry to those who I have missed. You are in my heart.

Jacqui Morris, Belinda Fitzpatrick, Dave Fanning, and Daryl Corletto - The best of Aussie mates. So glad that Kev didn't sour your Brophy experience and you are now our dear friends.

Leigh Ann Farrant & Sandi McNamara - Leigh, you were the first person I saw after I found out. Thank you for holding me. Sandi, thank you for supporting me after the news. Forever indebted.

My Irish family - So many to mention, so dear to my heart. I love you so much.

Benny, Gav, Loy, Wados, Keir, Wes, Cooper, Mickah, Kham, Carla, Jaya, Emma, Emily, Amy, Tara, AK, and Emma - I'm so blessed to have such amazing friends.

Mum and Dad - My beautiful parents. I can't unhear your cries. I can only gift you the tissue of my words. He loved you so much and he died the happiest he ever was. I know this is little solace but he smiles in the eyes of your grandkids. I love you so much.

Linda (Pins) and Aido - I have been blessed to be your elder brother. Although my guidance may have been more about what not to do in life. Kev would be so proud of you both. I know I am. I love you both so deeply.

Jacinta and Shaun - My dear sister-in-law, Kev misses your schnitzels! Shaun, his Casino partner in crime. Love you both dearly.

Alana, Leah, Olivia, Ava, and Connor - My amazing nieces and nephew, Kev would have been your favourite Uncle for sure. Watching you grow into the most amazing humans is a blessing.

Bruce, Margaret, Michelle, Anth, Olive, Henry, and Pearl - Thank you for welcoming me into your family. Love you guys...am I up for parole soon?

My kiddos - Zara Charlotte Brophy and Quinn Kevin Brophy - You are my world. The spring in my step. The pulse in my heart. My master teachers. I love you with a love that heals all wounds. Dadda

Kirsty Ann Lindsay - My beautiful soulmate. I loved you from the moment I saw you...even though I may have been trying to pick up your friend. We have seen the world. Rode the peaks of bliss. Waded through the troughs of darkness. And always side by side. You are my everything.

Kevin Anthony Brophy, aka Kebbles - You always did want your name in the liner notes of our favourite band's music. Sorry mate but this is as close as I could get. I love you, dear brother.

www.ingramcontent.com/pod-product-compliance
Lightning Source LLC
Chambersburg PA
CBHW070311010526
44107CB00056B/2561